Volcanoes of the World™

Tambora
A Killer From
Indonesia

Kathy Furgang

The Rosen Publishing Group's
PowerKids Press™
New York

For Uncle Dan

Published in 2001 by The Rosen Publishing Group, Inc.
29 East 21st Street, New York, NY 10010

First Edition

Series and Book Design: Michael Caroleo

Photo Credits: P. 1 courtesy of Royal Geographic Society; pp. 4, 16 (sun), 20 CORBIS; p. 7 (Illustration) by Michael Caroleo; pp. 8, 9, 12 Photodisc; pp. 11, 15 © Photri; p. 16 (crops) © International Stock; p. 19 © Michael S. Yamashita/CORBIS.

Furgang, Kathy.
    Tambora : a killer volcano from Indonesia / by Kathy Furgang.—1st ed.
      p. cm.— (Volcanoes of the world)
    Includes index.
    ISBN 0-8239-5661-X (alk. paper)
    1. Tambora, Mount (Indonesia)—Juvenile literature. 2. Volcanoes—Indonesia—Sumbawa—Juvenile literature. [1. Tambora, Mount (Indonesia) 2. Volcanoes.] I. Title.

QE523.T285 F87 2000
551.21'09598'6—dc21   00-028584

Manufactured in the United States of America

Contents

Tambora is on the island of Sumbawa in Indonesia. Indonesia is a group of small islands that lie southeast of Asia. Indonesia separates the Indian and Pacific Oceans.

Islands in the Sea

Tambora, one of the most famous and powerful volcanoes in the world, is on the island of Sumbawa, Indonesia. Indonesia is made up of more than 13,500 small islands. Only half of the islands actually have people living on them. Most of the islands are very small. Indonesia is a part of the continent of Asia. Indonesia lies in the Pacific and Indian Oceans, between Australia and the mainland of Asia. Many of Indonesia's islands have volcanoes on them. In 1815, Tambora made the biggest explosion of any volcano in recorded history! The explosion caused thousands of deaths. It affected people all around the world. Volcanoes are a constant reminder of how powerful nature can be.

A Volcano Forms

To understand volcanoes, you must understand what is inside Earth. Earth is made up of three layers. We live on the outside layer, called the **crust**. This layer is made of solid rock. The **mantle** is the layer below the crust. It is 1,800 miles (2,900 km) deep. It is made up of solid and liquid rock. It also contains different kinds of **minerals**. The very center of Earth is the **core**. The outer core is made of hot liquid rock. The center of the core is solid metal. Pressure makes the core so hot that it heats the entire mantle. Sometimes the mantle becomes so hot that some of its rock melts and becomes liquid. This liquid rock is called **magma**. A volcano is a break in Earth's crust where hot magma, gases, and ash from the mantle escape to the surface.

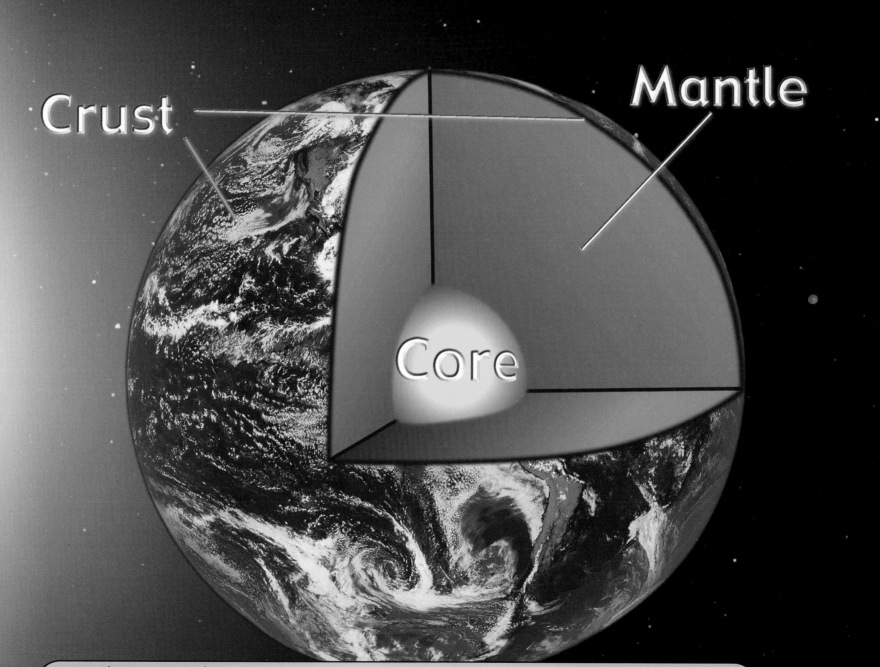

Earth's crust is about 5 to 25 miles (8 to 40 km) deep. The mantle is 1,800 miles (2,900 km) deep! Earth's core is a ball about 2,500 miles (3,460 km) across.

In a volcanic eruption, magma shoots up through cracks in the crust. When it reaches the surface it becomes lava. Tambora was made from cooled lava.

Breaking Through Earth!

It takes a very long time for a volcano to form on Earth's surface. Earth's crust is made of very large pieces of land called **plates**. Earth's plates move very slowly. Most of the time we can't feel this movement. Some plates move about four inches (10.3 cm) each year. Tambora was formed when the edges of two plates crunched together. This made a break in the crust. Over thousands of years, hot magma from the mantle escaped through the crack and shot up to the surface of Earth. When this happens it is called an eruption. Magma that reaches the surface of Earth is called **lava**. When lava cools, it becomes hard. Tambora is made of lava.

The Ring of Fire

The Pacific Ocean has more volcanoes than any other place on Earth. Most of the volcanoes on Earth were formed around the borders of great plates under the Pacific Ocean. This group of volcanoes is called the Ring of Fire. One of the volcanoes in the Ring of Fire is Tambora. Tambora started forming on the bottom of the ocean floor. Each eruption of lava hardened to form rock. The next layer of lava hardened on top of the last layer and a mound of rock was formed. Slowly, over a very long time, the mound of rock built up and reached out of the ocean to form a mountain. Volcanoes that form this way are called **stratovolcanoes**.

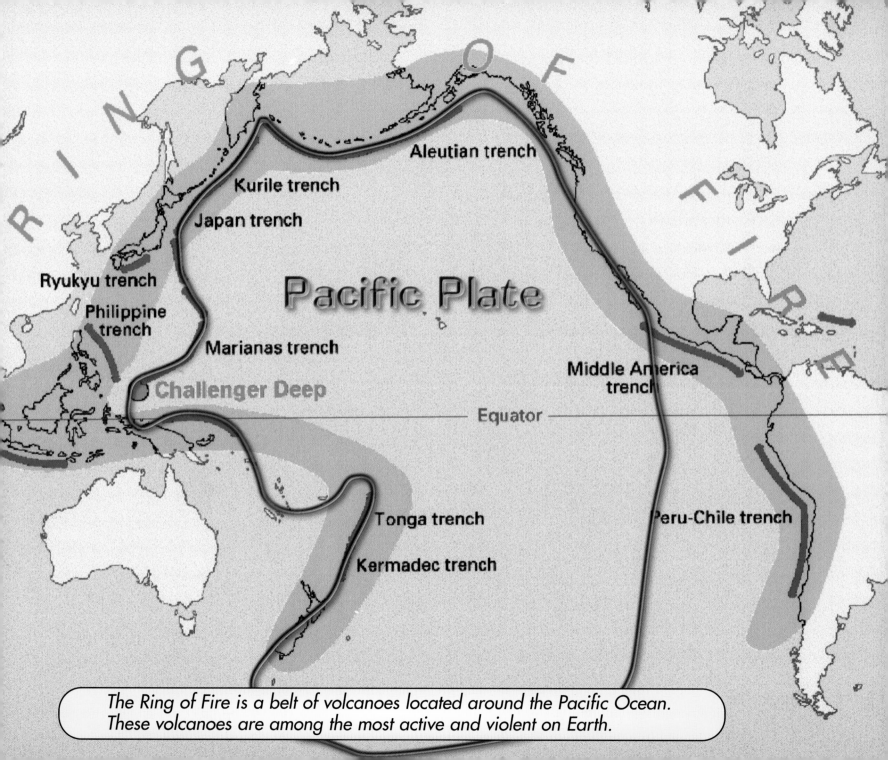

The Ring of Fire is a belt of volcanoes located around the Pacific Ocean.
These volcanoes are among the most active and violent on Earth.

When Tambora erupted in 1815, giant clouds of steam and smoke were blown miles (km) into the air.

Eruption of 1815

On April 10, 1815, Tambora exploded with the biggest eruption ever recorded. There was very little warning beforehand. Giant clouds of smoke, steam, and ash flew out of the opening at the top of the mountain. This opening is called a vent. All volcanoes have a vent at the top where magma can escape from Earth's crust. The ash and rock was blown miles (km) into the air. Ash fell as far as 800 miles (1,287 km) away from the volcano. Before the eruption, the mountain may have been as tall as 13,000 feet (3,962 m). During the eruption, a 4,000-foot (1,219 m) chunk of rock at the top of the mountain blew off. The eruption lasted several days. It changed the mountain forever.

Death and Damage

The 1815 eruption of Tambora was huge. The dangerous burning ash destroyed all of the land around the volcano. It also destroyed everything that lived on the island. More than 10,000 people were killed immediately by the blast. Another 82,000 people died later from the lack of food and from disease. The volcano burned the crops. Water supplies were flooded with mud. The water was filled with bacteria that made people ill. The blast was so big that the mountain itself changed. When the top of the mountain was blown off, it formed a **crater**. A crater formed by a volcano is called a **caldera**. Tambora's caldera is seen by **satellites** in the sky. It is four miles (6.43 km) across and 3,164 feet (1,109 m) deep.

14

The crater that was formed on top of Mount Tambora after the 1815 eruption is so large that it can be seen by satellites in the sky.

This picture shows ash blocking the sun during a volcanic eruption. Crops and water supplies can also be damaged by falling ash.

The Year Without a Summer

Not only did the eruption of Tambora cause death in Indonesia, it also affected people halfway around the world. The ash made such a thick cloud that it blocked some of the sun's light and heat! Ash from the eruption was blown 10 to 30 miles (16.1 to 48.3 km) into the air. It blocked the sun. This caused problems worldwide. For several months, the weather became colder in many places around Earth. The colder weather prevented crops from growing, even as far away as the United States. Some areas in New England had frost and snow in the months of June and July. The year of 1815 was called "The Year Without a Summer."

What We Know Now

Imagine living in 1815. People had to grow their own food. Today we get our food in stores. If a large volcano erupts today, news travels fast and people from all around the world can pitch in to help those in need. Airplanes can bring food to people who are starving. Scientists are now able to tell when some volcanoes might erupt. These scientists are called **volcanologists**. One tool they use is called a **seismometer**. It measures the movement of Earth and can tell when a volcano may be ready to erupt. With this information, people have more time to move to a safer place.

A volcanologist reads a seismograph, which measures Earth's movements. Seismographs can help tell where or when an eruption might occur.

This picture of islands in Indonesia was taken by satellite. The large island at the right of the picture has a volcano that is erupting.

Will Tambora Strike Again?

Earth is always changing. Volcanoes like Tambora are always changing, too. Will Tambora ever erupt again as it did in 1815? No one can tell for sure. Scientists can only keep track of changes that occur on the mountain. There has not been a large eruption of Tambora since 1815. Although volcanoes can be dangerous, they can also be helpful to Earth. Millions of years ago, volcanoes were responsible for creating Earth's oceans and atmosphere. Now certain crops, like coffee, depend on rich volcanic soil.

What About Other Planets?

Scientists have discovered that Earth is not the only planet in the solar system that has volcanoes. The solar system contains the nine planets, including Earth, that revolve around the Sun. The planet Mars may have the largest active volcano in the solar system. This volcano is called Olympus Mons. It is 375 miles (600 km) across and 15 miles (25 km) high, and it is still growing. By studying volcanoes on other planets, scientists can learn more about the volcanoes on Earth.

Glossary

caldera (kal-DEHR-ah) A crater formed by a volcano.

core (KOR) The hot center layer of Earth that is made of liquid and solid iron and other elements.

crater (KRAY-ter) A hole in the ground shaped like a bowl.

crust (KRUST) Earth's top layer of solid rock on which we live.

extinct (ik-STINKT) To no longer exist.

lava (LAH-vuh) A hot liquid made of melted rock that comes out of a volcano.

magma (MAG-muh) Hot liquid rock found in the mantle of Earth.

mantle (MAN-tul) The middle layer of Earth that lies between the core and the crust of Earth's surface.

minerals (MIH-ner-ulz) A natural ingredient from Earth's soil that is not a plant, animal, or other living thing.

plates (PLAYTS) The moving pieces of Earth's crust.

satellites (SA-til-yts) Machines in space that are used to predict weather.

seismometer (syz-MAH-meh-ter) An instrument used to measure the movement in Earth.

stratovolcano (strah-toh-vohl-KAY-noh) A volcano that is formed by many layers of lava.

volcanologists (vol-kuh-NOL-uh-jists) Scientists who study volcanoes.

23

Index

Web Sites

To find out more about Tambora and volcanoes, check out these Web sites:
http://volcano.und.nodak.edu/vwdocs/kids/kids.html
http://volcano.und.nodak.edu/vwdocs/volc_images/
southeast_asia/indonesia/tambora.html

24